D1372882

SOLVING REAL-WORLD PROBLEMS WITH AEROSPACE ENGINEERING

SELMA ISTAKHOROV

Britannica
Educational Publishing

IN ASSOCIATION WITH

ROSEN
EDUCATIONAL SERVICES

Published in 2016 by Britannica Educational Publishing (a trademark of Encyclopædia Britannica, Inc.) in association with The Rosen Publishing Group, Inc.
29 East 21st Street, New York, NY 10010

Distributed exclusively by Rosen Publishing.
To see additional Britannica Educational Publishing titles, go to rosenpublishing.com.

First Edition

Britannica Educational Publishing
J.E. Luebering: Director, Core Reference Group
Mary Rose McCudden: Editor, Britannica Student Encyclopedia

Rosen Publishing
Jacob R. Steinberg: Editor
Nelson Sá: Art Director
Nicole Russo: Designer
Cindy Reiman: Photography Manager
Karen Huang: Photo Researcher

Library of Congress Cataloging-in-Publication Data

Istakhorov, Selma, author.
Solving real-world problems with aerospace engineering / Selma Istakhorov.
    pages cm. — (Let's find out. Engineering)
Includes bibliographical references and index.
Audience: Grades 1–4.
ISBN 978-1-68048-263-8 (library bound) — ISBN 978-1-5081-0073-7 (pbk.) — ISBN 978-1-68048-320-8 (6-pack)
1. Aerospace engineering—Juvenile literature. I. Title.

TL793.I845 2016
629.1—dc23

2015026727

Manufactured in the United States of America

CONTENTS

LET'S SOAR!

The word *aerospace* describes Earth's **atmosphere** and the region beyond it called outer space. Aerospace therefore contains everything above Earth's surface, including the sky, the clouds, the stars, and other planets.

Aerospace engineers invent, build, and test vehicles that fly through the atmosphere

Aerospace engineering is the field that designs airplanes, spaceships, satellites, and more.

> **Atmosphere** describes the whole mass of air (or gases) that surrounds a planet.

and those that fly into outer space. Those vehicles include airplanes, missiles, space shuttles, and satellites.

Aerospace engineering is one field, or type, of engineering. Engineers design products that can solve economic, environmental, or social problems. Aerospace engineering solves economic and environmental problems both on Earth and in outer space. Solving these problems

Aerospace engineers build and test satellites such as this one that was launched into space in late 2009.

◀◀

Aerospace engineers design, build, and inspect the different parts of an aircraft.

helps the world become a better, cleaner, and safer place. It also makes it easier to travel and to collect and share information.

All engineers use physics, math, and chemistry to develop new products or to improve the things we already have. An aerospace engineer must have strong knowledge of all three subjects. They use math to make calculations such as how much fuel is needed to allow an aircraft to travel a certain distance. Aerospace

Think About It

What are some tasks you can think of that are easier to do with the help of aerospace engineering?

engineers study chemistry to learn about different materials that can be used to build spacecraft or how chemicals can be combined to make the fuel needed to power a spacecraft. Aerospace engineers use their understanding of physics to think about such things

as how the shape of an aircraft can allow the aircraft to travel easily through the air. Because there are so many different things to think about, aerospace engineers usually work in one particular area.

ARE WE THERE YET?

Airplanes are the most common way to travel by air. There are two types of airplanes: civil airplanes and military airplanes. Civil airplanes are ones used for travel by regular passengers. When you go on vacation, you fly in a civil airplane. Mail services also use these planes to carry mail over long distances. Military airplanes are those used by armed forces such as the air force and the army.

Civil airplanes are the ones regular passengers fly in to visit family or to go on vacation.

Two brothers named Orville and Wilbur Wright invented the first powered airplane in 1905. Since then, airplanes have increased in speed from about 40 miles (64 kilometers) per hour to more than 550 miles (885 km) per hour. The fastest that most cars can safely travel on highways is 60 or 70 miles (97 or 112 km) per hour. At those speeds, a car trip from New York to Florida takes 20 hours. Airplanes can make that trip in just three hours!

Orville Wright flies an airplane he built with his brother in Fort Myer, Virginia, in 1908.

Think About It

Why do you think it is important for the military to have airplanes that travel quickly?

THE SPACE FRONTIER

No frontier has inspired humans' imagination like outer space. In the first half of the 20th century, space travel seemed like a fantasy. It appeared only in science fiction books and movies. Few believed that technology would move forward as quickly as it did in just a half a century.

Starting in the 1950s, aerospace engineers in the United States and the Soviet Union worked to build vehicles that could travel into outer space. (The Soviet Union was a country that existed from 1922 to 1991. Part of that country is now Russia.) On October 4, 1957, the Soviet Union launched *Sputnik 1*, the first man-made satellite. The Soviet Union also sent the first human into space, in 1961. Eight years later, on July 20, 1969, two US astronauts were the first humans to land on the moon. On June 13, 1983, the US space probe *Pioneer 10* became the first man-made

> A **space station** is a satellite that stays in orbit around Earth. It lets astronauts stay in space for long periods of time and perform science experiments.

object to travel outside our solar system.

Another major advance in space technology came in 1971. That year the Soviet Union launched the world's first **space station**, Salyut 1. In 1986 Soviet aerospace engineers launched another space station

The US space probe *Pioneer 10* was launched in 1972.

called Mir. Mir stayed open until 2000. During that time more than 100 people, including some US astronauts, spent time on board the space station.

In 1981 the United States launched the first of a series of space shuttles that could go to outer space

The Russian space station Mir can be seen flying over New Zealand as it orbited Earth in 1996.

THINK ABOUT IT

What are some aircraft or spacecraft from science fiction books or movies today that aerospace engineering might actually invent in the future?

In July 2006, the US space shuttle *Discovery* lifted off on one of its trips to outer space.

and return many times. In January 1986, the *Challenger* space shuttle exploded on launch. The United States stopped its space program until it knew it could safely send astronauts to space. In 1988 the program continued. Shuttle astronauts helped build the International Space Station beginning in 1998. The space station was shared by 16 countries. The last shuttle flight took place in 2011.

WEATHER SATELLITES

One great invention to come out of aerospace engineering is the weather satellite. A weather satellite is used to predict the weather, or to tell what the weather will be like. Satellites are small objects that revolve around a larger object in space. Some satellites are natural, such as the moon, which revolves around Earth. Others are artificial, or made by people. Weather satellites are artificial satellites.

Aerospace engineers design and build weather satellites. These satellites help scientists study the weather. They also have cameras to take pictures of

Earth. Weather satellites track the location of clouds. They also measure the temperatures of Earth's land and oceans. Weather satellites carry sensors that send information about weather conditions back to Earth.

Aerospace engineers must have knowledge of mechanics, paths, force, speed, and the spacecraft industry. With this knowledge, they can design and build artificial satellites such as weather satellites. With the help of aerospace engineering, we can correctly predict the weather—both good and bad!

Weather satellites help track changing weather patterns such as hurricanes.

NAVIGATION

A GPS satellite is another exciting example of an aerospace engineering invention. GPS stands for Global Positioning System. It is a **navigation** and location tool. A GPS satellite can give an object's exact location by latitude, longitude, and altitude. Aerospace engineers build GPS satellites for both military and civilian use. These satellites circle Earth

Navigation is the science of getting vehicles such as ships, aircraft, and spacecraft from place to place.

A GPS satellite in orbit over Earth can detect the exact location of an object.

16

and send radio signals to a GPS receiver on Earth. Using mathematical calculations, a GPS receiver can measure the distance between itself and the GPS satellite.

GPS satellites are used to help airplanes, spacecraft, and even space stations navigate. Aerospace engineers work hard to make sure these satellites send information quickly and accurately. This information can prevent accidents such as airplane crashes from happening. If there is a technical problem with a satellite, aerospace engineers must figure out the problem and quickly fix it.

A solar-powered GPS system measures the strength of earthquakes in Santorini, Greece.

EXPLORATION

Aerospace engineering is also responsible for building spacecraft to collect information about other planets. Scientists are especially interested in studying Mars. They want to learn if there is life on Mars and if humans could survive there. Mars's atmosphere is different from Earth's, and spacecraft must be designed to operate well there.

The Soviet Union first launched a spacecraft toward Mars in 1962, but it failed to land on the planet. In 1971

The planet Mars is often seen as the next frontier for human exploration in outer space.

The *Viking* probes were the first US spacecraft to operate on the surface of Mars.

the Soviet Union successfully landed its first spacecraft on Mars. In 1976 the United States successfully launched its *Viking* probes to Mars. Since then, many more advanced spacecraft have landed on the planet.

In 1997, the Mars Pathfinder released the first rover onto Mars's surface. This rover collected data for three months. Since then, several more rovers have landed on Mars. Rovers are used to perform experiments on Mars's soil and atmosphere.

THINK ABOUT IT

In 2015, scientists found evidence that liquid water runs on Mars. What effects could this have on human exploration of the planet?

Going Green!

Thousands of pieces of space junk are in orbit around Earth. The junk is the remains of satellites, spaceships, and other materials that were sent into space but are no longer used. This material can be as large as a discarded rocket stage or as small as a tiny chip of paint. Space junk can damage other satellites and spacecraft and even an astronaut's spacesuit or helmet.

This piece of space junk (about two inches [five centimeters] long) is a by-product of spacecraft rocket motors.

Aerospace engineers are trying to come up with ways to clean up this garbage. Engineers in Japan invented a steel cable called a tether. This tether would be attached to a satellite. It would act as a net to collect metal objects that are floating in space. Other aerospace engineers have suggested such plans as using lasers to clear away the junk or sending robots to collect the extra materials.

Aerospace engineers designed a special tether to collect space junk floating around Earth.

Think About It

What are some problems humans could face in the future if we do not clean up space junk?

Jobs in Aerospace Engineering

The field of aerospace engineering offers different jobs for people who want to work with aircraft and spacecraft. Aerospace engineers spend a lot of time solving problems and inventing new technology for flight vehicles.

Aerospace engineers may be either aeronautical engineers or astronautical engineers. Aeronautical engineers work with airplanes, helicopters, and other aircraft. Astronautical engineers work with satellites, rockets, and spacecraft.

There are different areas that aerospace

Astronautical engineers design, build, and test vehicles for space exploration.

engineers must work in. Aerodynamics involves the study of airflow over vehicles. It helps engineers design vehicles that can lift off the ground and fly through the air safely.

COMPARE AND CONTRAST

What do aerodynamics engineers and aircraft design engineers have in common? How are their jobs different?

Another area in which aerospace engineers work is the design of aircraft structures. These engineers design vehicles to serve a specific purpose and withstand forces encountered during flight. Such engineers may be experts in commercial planes, military fighters, or helicopters.

Aeronautical engineers are experts at designing and building aircraft that are safe and useful.

23

FAMOUS FIGURES IN AEROSPACE ENGINEERING

Many aerospace engineers are famous for their achievements. The builder of the first airplane model was Samuel Pierpont Langley. On May 6, 1896, Langley flew a strange-looking machine near Washington, DC. It was about 16 feet (5 meters) long and weighed 26 pounds (12 kilograms). The craft flew about a half a mile in about one and a half minutes. This was the first time a machine heavier than air flew for more than just a few seconds. (His craft did not have a person .

THE AERODROME AS SEEN FROM ABOVE.

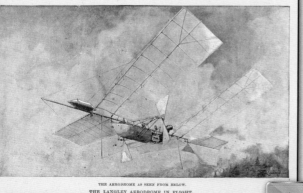

THE AERODROME AS SEEN FROM BELOW.
THE LANGLEY AERODROME IN FLIGHT.

These drawings show Samuel Pierpont Langley's unmanned steam-powered aerodrome.

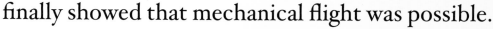

Leroy Grumman (*left*) designed advanced military aircraft and spacecraft for the United States.

on board.) After doing many experiments in the laboratory, he finally showed that mechanical flight was possible.

Leroy Randle Grumman was another famous aerospace engineer. Grumman was a flight instructor and later a test pilot before becoming an aerospace engineer. He designed military aircraft during World War II. He designed many planes that were very successful. His company even designed the spacecraft that first brought humans to the moon.

COMPARE AND CONTRAST

Do you think Langley's or Grumman's achievements were more important for aerospace engineering? Why?

LOOKING AHEAD!

Studying Martian clouds helps scientists understand the atmosphere—and if it can support life or not.

One of the most exciting areas of aerospace engineering is studying the possibility of life in outer space. More advanced spacecraft are being built to study other planets in Earth's solar system, as well as planets in other solar systems. One major area of interest is finding alien life. If scientists can find life on another planet, then maybe humans can survive on that planet, too!

Alien life is life that comes from or exists outside Earth and its atmosphere.

Many scientists believe that some form of life might exist on Mars. Mars has a lot in common with Earth. It has clouds, weather patterns, and polar ice caps just like our planet. Past missions have looked for evidence of living organisms on Mars. Today, scientists are trying to learn if humans could live there. Aerospace engineers are working to design buildings that humans could live in on Mars. Aerospace engineers are always looking ahead to the future.

ENGINEERING IN ACTION

Now that you have learned all about aerospace engineering, you can put it into practice. In this activity, the goal is to design a model parachute. The parachute must fly smoothly and land safely.

A successful parachute needs a large canopy (the parachute's fabric roof). This will help it stay in the air longer and fall slowly. The bigger the diameter or width of the canopy, the more air the parachute can catch. For this activity you

A parachute's canopy is what allows it to float slowly—and safely—to the ground.

can use different sized coffee filters. You can test which size works best for the model parachute.

The parachute's canopy is attached to the load (the person or object the parachute carries) by suspension lines. Try cutting different length pieces of string to attach the coffee filters to a small Lego or light toy. Use a hole punch to make two holes near opposite edges of the coffee filter. Tie each side of the filter to the toy. Test different canopy sizes and string lengths, and see how simple aerodynamics can make a small object fly. You're an aerospace engineer in training!

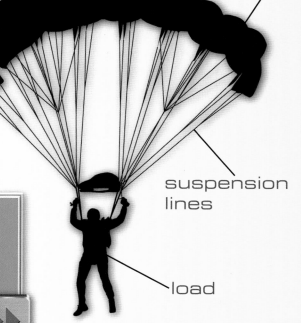

canopy

suspension lines

load

This diagram shows the parts of a parachute. Alter your model and see how the changes affect its flight.

GLOSSARY

achievements Goals reached or accomplishments gotten by effort.

altitude The vertical distance of an object above a given level (as sea level).

civil Of or relating to ordinary matters rather than to those of the military.

diameter A line segment through the center of a circle with its ends on the circle's circumference.

economic Of or relating to the making and buying of goods and services.

environmental Of or relating to all the physical surroundings on Earth.

experiments Procedures or operations carried out under controlled conditions to discover something, to test a hypothesis, or to serve as an example.

latitude Distance north or south from the equator measured in degrees.

launch To send off an object, especially with force.

longitude Distance measured by degrees or time east or west from the prime meridian.

mechanics A science that deals with energy and forces and their effect on bodies.

missiles Objects (such as a rocket) that are thrown, shot, or launched usually so as to strike something at a distance.

orbit To move in a circle around another object.

organisms Individual living things that carry on the activities of life by means of organs.

rover A robotic vehicle that explores the surface of a planet or other outer space object.

sensors Devices that detect a physical quantity (as a movement or a beam of light) and respond by transmitting a signal.

social Of or relating to human society or the relationships between members of a community.

technology The use of science in solving problems.

tether A line by which something is fastened so as to limit its range.

vehicles Things used to transport persons or goods.

FOR MORE INFORMATION

Books

Lassieur, A. *The Race to the Moon: An Interactive History Adventure.* North Mankato, MN: Capstone Press, 2014.

Rooney, A. *Aerospace Engineering and the Principles of Flight.* St. Catharines, ON: Crabtree Publishing Company, 2013.

Rooney, A. *Space Record Breakers.* Dubai, United Arab Emirates: Carlton Books, 2014.

Szumski, B. *Careers in Engineering.* San Diego, CA: ReferencePoint Press, 2015.

Websites

Because of the changing nature of Internet links, Rosen Publishing has developed an online list of websites related to the subject of this book. This site is updated regularly. Please use this link to access the list:

http://www.rosenlinks.com/LFO/Aero

INDEX